Families

Foster Parents

Rebecca Rissman

Heinemann Library
Chicago, Illinois

www.heinemannraintree.com

Visit our website to find out
more information about
Heinemann-Raintree books.

To order:

☎ Phone 888-454-2279

🖥 Visit www.heinemannraintree.com
to browse our catalog and order online.

Edited by Rebecca Rissman and Catherine Veitch
Designed by Ryan Frieson
Picture research by Tracy Cummins
Originated by Capstone Global Library Ltd
Printed and bound in China by Leo Paper Products Ltd

14 13 12 11 10
10 9 8 7 6 5 4 3 2 1

Library of Congress Cataloging-in-Publication Data

Rissman, Rebecca.
  Foster parents / Rebecca Rissman.
    p. cm.—(Families)
  Includes bibliographical references and index.
  ISBN 978-1-4329-4657-9 (hc)—ISBN 978-1-4329-4665-4 (pb)
1. Foster parents—Juvenile literature. 2. Foster children—Juvenile
literature. 3. Foster home care—Juvenile literature. 4. Families—
Juvenile literature. I. Title.
  HQ759.7.R58 2011
  306.874—dc22
                                          2010016992

Acknowledgments

We would like to thank the following for permission to reproduce
photographs: AP Photo pp. **11** (Imaginechina), **17** (John Froschauer);
Corbis pp. **4** (©David P. Hall), **6** (©Ann Summa), **8** (©Kevin Dodge),
15, **18** (©Edward Bock), **23c** (©David P. Hall); Getty Images pp.
5 (Tom Stoddar), **7** (Charlie Schuck), **10** (Jon Riley), **12** (Robert
Gallagher), **14** (DK Stock/David Deas), **21** (Camille Tokerud), **22**
(Jeremy Woodhouse), **23a** (Jon Riley); istockphoto pp. **9** (©Alexander
Shalamov), **19** (©Tomasz Markowski), **20** (©Aldo Murillo);
Shutterstock pp. **13** (©BlueOrange Studio), **16** (©Golden Pixels LLC),
23b (©BlueOrange Studio).

Front cover photograph of a family by a lake reproduced with
permission of Getty Images (Robert Gallagher). Back cover
photograph of a mother and child reproduced with permission of
Shutterstock (©BlueOrange Studio).

We would like to thank Anne Pezalla and Nancy Harris for their
invaluable help in the preparation of this book.

Every effort has been made to contact copyright holders of
any material reproduced in this book. Any omissions will
be rectified in subsequent printings if notice is given to
the publisher.

Contents

What Is a Family?

A family is a group of people.
People in families are called
family members.

The people in families care for
each other.

All families are different.

All families are special.

What Are Families Like?

Some families are big.

Some families are small.

What Is Foster Care?

Foster care makes sure children are cared for.

Foster care puts children with
new families.

Who Are Foster Parents?

Foster children's new parents are called foster parents.

Foster parents care for the children.

Some foster parents care for children for a long time.

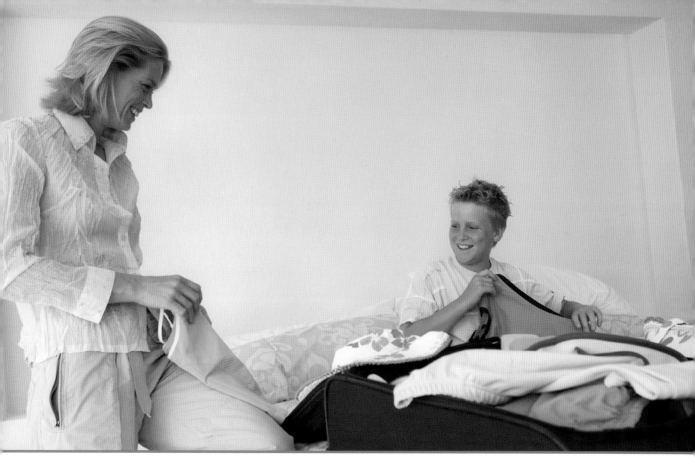

Some foster parents care for children for a short time.

Some foster parents care for
one child.

Some foster parents care for more than one child.

Children Living with Foster Parents

Some foster parents care for children who have been hurt.

Foster parents care for children whose parents could not care for them.

Some children leave their
foster parents to live with their
(20) parents again.

Some children leave their foster
parents to live with new families.

Do You Know?

Do you know any foster parents?

Picture Glossary

foster care helps keep children safe and cared for

foster parent adult who looks after children that are not their own

member person who belongs to a group

Index

Note to Parents and Teachers
Before Reading
Explain to children that foster care is a special system that makes sure all children are cared for and safe. Some children are in foster care for a short time, and then return to their families. Other children are in foster care until they can be adopted by new families. Explain that adoption is a system that places children with new families.

After Reading
Discuss with children how foster parents help children in need. Some children in foster care require special attention that their parents may not have been able to give to them. Other children in foster care were not able to live with their parents because they were unsafe.

24